NOT BROKEN
Just Refined

NOT BROKEN
Just Refined

Erica Estella

DEDICATION

My children were and are my lifeline during this entire rebirthing. They have motivated me to keep moving and not give up on my dreams, happiness, and love.

When I wanted to die,
RTJ *revived me.*

When I wanted to give up,
RTJ *motivated me.*

When I couldn't breathe,
RTJ *made me exhale.*

When I didn't have hope,
RTJ*'s faces showed me God truly lives.*

RTJ, it is an honor to be your mother. I don't take that title for granted. You three are my driving force for finishing this book so I can heal and help others in this situation.

My babies, thank you for loving me and believing in me when I didn't. You are the reason I continue to live, thrive, work because you three fuel my soul to never give up. Thank you for being my blessings.

ACKNOWLEDGEMENTS

My faith was tested during the dark days. I have come to realization that **GOD** is my all in all through the good, bad, and okay days. I don't know where I would be without HIM. I know my road will not be a straight one, yet I feel free and at peace with my choices moving forward. I will have U-turns, slippery slopes, and do not enter signs but I will continue to ground myself in the Word. I can't, and I won't do it without my Lord and Savior. I relinquish my power to GOD so He can work in me. He has given a new heart and a new peace. I still don't understand the refreshing and calmness I feel after this storm.

Mom, you showed me so much grace and love during my entire life. During my divorce I saw a different side of you. I felt your prayers, I saw your encouragement, and my pain was your pain. My tears became your tears, your strength became my strength. I was so grateful that you came to help me and continue to help me. Mommy, I love you.

Deacon Johnson, **Mrs. Johnson** and my **church family**, thank you for holding my hands spiritually on this new chapter of my life. Without prejudice to my situation this helped me believe and know that GOD was on my side. My faith has grown so much during this transition.

My **CORE** has held me down through this entire process. When I was getting married my aunt said, "Never stop having your real friends around, you never know when you're going to need them." She was so right. Thank you for loving me on my worst and broke days. I was emotional, vulnerable, and hopeful for having you. I appreciate you all.

My **Scribe Coach, Penda L. James**. You were a vital component to bringing my story alive. I appreciate your mentorship on how you made me think logically through this phase and to bring forth my life in a most authentic way. Your motivation and eagerness to not let me quit is why I am here today.

Erica Estella, you are not broken, but refined completely. You have started to believe in yourself again, you have started to love yourself more. You have started to realize that you are enough, that you are worth loving.

You now know that God didn't make a mistake with you or your journey in life. You are here to be uncomfortable; you will grow and change the dynamic of your life.

Don't ever forget that.

FOREWORD

God's word is true when He says in II Corinthians 8-10, "My strength is perfected in your weakness."

I met Erica and her ex-husband in 2019, shortly after joined the church where I serve as a Deacon. As the Deacon assigned to support them, it was my responsibility to provide spiritual guidance and help them navigate the challenges they might face in a large congregation. I was immediately impressed with the love they had for each other, and their three children and I believed they would be a great addition to our church family. Her partner became very active in the mass choir, and she was always by his side supporting him.

A few years after they joined Erica confided in me that her partner was seeing a man and contemplating leaving her for that relationship. Because I had not seen anything that would lead me to think they had anything but a loving union, this announcement weighed on me. I prayed with her, we spoke at length about her situation, and she shared with me how it impacted her as a woman. But most of all I made myself available to just listen. Erica's fortitude and strength in dealing with a situation that may have devastated another woman demonstrates her strong faith in God.

I hope you will be inspired by Erica's willingness to share her story, especially if you are going through your own trial. You are not weak; God's strength is perfected in you.

~Joe Johnson, Church Deacon
Georgia

CONTENTS

Foreword vii

Love At First Sight 1

Mr. And Mrs. 3

Becoming Parents.. 11

Changes, Changes... 15

Milestones 19

Transitions... 25

Hello, Georgia.. 33

2019 Rain 41

2021... 45

True Colors 61

Open and Closed.. 66

Divorce Hurts Children, Too............................. 84

the woman in me.. 92

Betrayal 96

Unraveling 104

On the Other Side... 108

The Beginning of the End 118

Refined... 120

References 130

Moments Of Refinement..132

Songs Of Refinement..134

LOVE AT FIRST SIGHT

"Who is that fine boy over there?"

When I first saw my ex-husband, J, he was playing the lion in *The Wiz*. He was so cute; he looked like a big teddy bear. He attended an all-boys high school, and I attended an all-girls high school. The schools interacted with each other in joint choirs, drama club and the decathlon team. J was in the joint choir and the drama club. Oh my God, J can sing! His magical voice once soothed me.

I was an athlete in high school. If it wasn't about basketball or hanging out with my friends at school, you heard nothing from me. For that reason, I sent my friend who was a senior to ask J for his number. I was a shy freshman and didn't have the confidence to talk to him. I knew she could do it because she was a senior. When she returned with J's number, I was as excited as I would have been if I had won the big payout in a lottery!

We started to talk on the phone every night. We talked about everything. I even skipped basketball practice to go be in his presence. J wasn't the type of guy I usually fell for. First, he loved and respected his grandmother, and mother and most of all he loved God. He was not athletic, but he was a scholar. For our first date he picked me up from my house and my Belizean parents approved of him before I knew I was going to approve of him. We cleaned up his church which wasn't bad, but I had never been on a date like that.

J and I dated exclusively through high school. We went to each other's school prom and for graduation we celebrated with each other's families. After high school J went to Loyola Marymount University (LMU) with his best friend, I knew his roommate, too, he was his best friend from high school. I attended EL Camino College and grew into a collegiate athlete on the basketball team.

My second year in college I started to work at Centinela Hospital to get experience in the medical field. My boss gave me the opportunity to get trained as a Telemetry Technician and I monitored the hearts on the Cardiac Unit. Usually after my shift I would drive to LMU to see J. It made me happy that J and his roommate had a history of friendship, he wasn't alone at school.

MR. AND MRS.

After five years of dating, J asked both of our parents to give their blessing and he asked for my hand in marriage. On my birthday in 2005, J took me on an incredible date at Gladstone's, a restaurant in Long Beach, California. After dinner, the waitress brought a big martini glass filled with cotton candy. I saw the engagement ring on top of the tray. J got up from his seat, got on one knee, and asked, "Will you marry me?"

I remember the tan suit he was wearing that night. I can still see the sweat bullets on his face, and his sexy brown eyes looking deeply into my soul waiting for my response. I had no other answer, so I said, "YES!" I was hopeful about marrying the man I loved since high school. I couldn't ask God for anything else; I thought I was complete.

We continued our celebration. We went on a getaway to a luxury camping site in Santa Barbara called "El Capitan." We went swimming in the outside pool, bike riding where I fell and J, made sure I was okay; we continued enjoying each other.

After a year of planning for our wedding, I finally became J's wife on August 12, 2006. Everything was amazing. The church was beautiful. My godmother and family did all the decorations. Our wedding party looked so magical. The bridesmaids wore pastel colored dresses, while the groomsmen had on slick black tuxedos. J's best friend was the best man at our wedding.

I was in a dream as the doors opened to the sanctuary and I saw my best friend, my lover, my soon-to-be husband. I was extremely excited and nervous to have J see me for the first time as his wife. The church was full to capacity, everyone seemed to be happy and excited for our matrimony.

Honeymoon

As we prepared for our honeymoon, to Catalina Island I looked towards the future and watched the ocean waves, and blue California sky roll past me. It was a perfect day. We drove to Long Beach where we had to take a ferry boat to the Island. This was J and I first time on the island so we were ready to explore and make memories that would definitely last a lifetime. We saw that golf carts were for rent so we wanted to rent one so we could explore the entire island, but we were too young; we had to be 25 years of age. J and I both read the sign and we laughed like, "well, let the walking begin."

Adjusting to Marriage

In the early years of my marriage, I was the kind of wife who checked in to make sure everything was okay with us. I never wanted to be oblivious of things happening in my relationship; I didn't turn my head when it felt like something was off between us. I always asked hard questions and raised issues. J used to think that I was being controlling, but I thought I was being proactive, alert, and informed. I always acknowledged the elephant in the room.

Even though we were young, married, and didn't have a dime to our name, we had love, dreams, and aspirations to be great. We supported each other in everything. I valued J's opinion and I strived to be his best friend.

Family Support

I am thankful for our parents who supported our marriage in many ways. My parents allowed me to shop in their kitchen and were always willing to help us. J's mother treated me like her own daughter. We lived with her, saved money, and paid off debt. She opened her home and allowed us to move in until we found our own place a year into our marriage. We were excited when we moved into our first apartment in Hawthorne on Yukon and Rosecrans Ave. I got furniture, kitchen utensils and of course, a bed because I was ready to enjoy intimacy with no restrictions. You know I couldn't scream and moan at my love-in-law the way I wanted to.

Intimacy

J had told me one time that he was molested at a young age. He never said anything about how it affected him or what he thought about it. His molestation was a non-factor to me until 2020, when it came up again.

When we had sex, I thought we were having great sex. I was J's first female sex partner so all he knew was me. I wish he would have had a little more experience, maybe he would have enjoyed having sex as much as I did. I wanted it all the time, morning, noon, and night. I was overly aroused, and I think sometimes I took advantage of J. I guess he didn't want to feel like less of a man by complaining about making love to me. I just went with the flow.

J didn't take initiative with sex, so I took the lead on sex in hopes of spicing things up for us. I would throw him onto the bed or against the wall, kiss him on his neck and all over until he was fully erect. When he was ready, I would devour him because I didn't know the next I would be able to eat. We could go weeks or months without having sex.

I would ask, "Why haven't we been intimate?"

J would always say, "I don't have a high sex drive because of the medication I am on for my diabetes and high blood pressure. I can't get in the mood." I put my needs and desires on hold to make him comfortable, but I deprived myself of the intimacy that I truly desired. If I laid in the bed naked, he would look and compliment me and fall asleep.

I wanted J to show his desire for me, to be adventurous with toys and drink my nectar. I wanted him to penetrate me hard and deep but I learned that he wanted the same thing, just not from me. It is sad that I couldn't satisfy him, and he couldn't satisfy me.

Our marriage was great. It was just that one aspect that was lacking; but was it enough to end the marriage? I think our relationship, our union was truly based on love and familiarity. It was my safe haven. I knew what I was getting, and my rewards were much more than what I was lacking.

Our First Home

In the meantime, J and I worked hard to fix our credit. We found an amazing realty team and paid off all of our debt. In 2012 we purchased our first home. I was so happy with our accomplishment—we had a piece of the American pie. We had so much faith in God that we solicited estimates for renovations before we closed on the escrow.

As soon as we moved in, we started putting our own touches on the house and making memories to last a lifetime. Adjusting into home ownership, we worked, paid bills, and hosted gatherings for our close family and friends at our home. It felt good to think that the fairytale of my life was falling into place; life was going great. J was my husband, my best friend, my helpmate, my everything.

J and I were both were active in our community and J ran for city office. Despite not winning, it was an experience for us to work on his campaign and canvass in our community. We did the work together and I was proud of our endeavors. I was pregnant with our third child, working a twelve-hour night shift and didn't mind standing at the corner with homemade signs that read, "Vote for J, let's change Compton."

Stranger

Live with you
Sleep with you
Smile and laugh with you
Stranger in you
Vow to love me
vow to protect me
Still it's you
A stranger in you

- Erica Estella

"It is my goal to make sure that my children have an amazing childhood."

~Erica Estella

BECOMING PARENTS

We added parenthood into our marriage and conceived our first daughter, R in Vegas in the hot tub. Honestly, every time we had passionate sex, we got pregnant. At home when the bed broke, we conceived T. Drunk in love with Hennessy we conceived J, Jr. I felt peace, love and happiness becoming a mother. I was even more eager to be successful and accomplish my dreams. I resumed my nursing classes because I wanted to help carry the load for my family. I got a job working overtime at Centinela Hospital. I worked there and went to school part-time for over 12 years, putting myself on the back burner. I tried school, working, being a wife and mom, it's a lot. I know many can do it, but it was a load on me.

One day while working on a report, my colleague and friend Jen smirked when she looked at me. She said, "Erica, you're pregnant!"

I was like, "Girl, please stop saying that. No, I am not." Throughout the 12-hour shift, she would randomly come to my station, look down at my stomach and repeat herself. I was getting annoyed because I didn't want to believe that I was pregnant. I had noticed that I was gaining weight, but I thought I was just happy. When I was feeling nauseated and lethargic, I thought it was a normal sickness. My period was late, so I caved in and bought several pregnancy tests. I took them and they were all positive!

"Wow, we are pregnant!" I thought. "How will I tell J, about this?" I was overly joyful and blessed to have a growing life within me.

I found an app called Pregnancy and Baby Tracker. I became obsessed with knowing the development and changes that were happening within my body. I loved watching the updates that she was growing from a small pea into a cantaloupe. I loved feeling the flutters and later, the jabs of her kicks during my pregnancy. I couldn't wait to hold her in my arms. March 16, 2010, I had the privilege of birthing our first child. I remember staring at her in amazement when we were in the recovery room.

My second pregnancy was rough because I was older and considered obese. The doctors discovered that I had fibroids during the pregnancy. The fibroids made it difficult to see the developing fetus. During several ultrasounds the medical staff mentioned that they couldn't see the baby's head development, and that made me worry.

My stress level increased but I had to lean on my faith and remain calm. I used to talk to God and think about the fact that my children do not belong to me, but to Him. I prayed, "If they die, it's because it is the plan You have for their lives." On August 16, 2013, after a challenging pregnancy, we welcomed our second daughter. She was a healthy nine pounds and 21 inches.

Everything changed for me after I gave birth to T. Having two small children really put my life into perspective. I had a job at an amazing hospital in Inglewood, California, yet I was investing so much in the facility and not receiving the pay I deserved. The cost of living was increasing while my pay was at a standstill. I advocated for a rate increase with meetings and a letter writing campaign to my managers. I started looking for employment with better opportunities for growth, better wages, and affordable benefits for our growing family. It is my goal to make sure that my children have an amazing childhood—I feel like I owe them that.

The second baby was born through a Cesarean procedure. I had limited mobility due to the pain of the surgery and staples in my abdomen. Being immobilized made me feel helpless, which I believe led to postpartum depression. I didn't want to do anything but sleep, I was feeling dull and uninterested in everything around me, especially my then husband and my children. I believe the depression hit me like a tidal wave. Everything hit me at one time. I was juggling marriage, two small children, and working full-time. I was making sure to be present for everyone else, but putting myself last and that was no longer working for me. I don't blame anyone but myself for my burnout, I was stretching myself thin.

Although J was amazing at taking care of me and our family, the thought of him touching me, for any reason, was revolting. "I am in this situation and in pain because of him getting me pregnant," I would think to myself. On one particular day after the baby was born, J tried to assist me in getting up from the couch, he reached to touch me. I would flinch because I didn't want to be touched.

When he reached for me, I snapped at him and pulled away. He said, "I'm here to help you, Erica! I could be at work." He huffed, "I don't need this!" His words stung and rang in my head like a bell. I woke the hell up after that. But I still needed time to adjust and heal. I let him help me up and I took a shower. In my alone time, I prayed, "God, help me get out from under this dark cloud of depression and revive my mind and energy to be able to take care of my children and myself."

CHANGES, CHANGES

In 2015, MKL Hospital opened in my neighborhood. I knew that I needed to serve at this new, state-of-the-art hospital where I lived and was raising my family. I truly wanted to grow in my career by giving back to the community through service. Being hired was a dream come true for me.

I enjoyed working at MKL, everyone made working to save lives their priority over getting paid. I was living in the moment of accomplishing something great, but I still had more to achieve like becoming a Registered Nurse (RN). It was hard to put time into myself, but I felt at times I was chasing a dream that would never be my reality. Year after year I watched people become nurses and I wished it was me too. Yes, I was happy for them, but I could not make myself a priority. It's like I was everyone's cheerleader except my own.

Slacking in my responsibilities was not just in pursuing my goals of becoming an RN. I was slacking with my health, too. I knew that heart disease and diabetes are prevalent in my family bloodline. I needed to take steps to make better choices and stay physically active. What would it have mattered if I had achieved all my goals and did not have good health?

I was borderline diabetic, considered morbidly obese and the weight was not coming off even though I wasn't on medication, and I worked out rigorously lifting weights, walking, jogging and dance classes to get my body in shape.

To reclaim my health, I asked my doctor about having gastric sleeve surgery. He sent me to classes that helped me learn how to rewire my mind about food. I worked out on a regular basis with my trainer before the surgery because I wanted to look as natural as possible. So, weightlifting and drills was my new regimen during this life transformation.

I was elated about the new chapter and looked forward to being transformed into a lighter, healthier me. Once I reshaped my mind and got into an emotionally stable and happy place, I was ready for my surgery.

In the process I learned that some individuals in my life did not want to see me change for the better. It hurt me that one of my close friends wasn't loving or supportive of me the way I loved her and our friendship. We used to do everything together. I used to jokingly call her husband my husband and her children were my godchildren.

Right after my surgery, when my friend saw my transformation, it was like she totally flipped her attitude toward me. First, she attacked me for getting the sleeve. "Don't you think working out was good enough?" she asked. "Why did you have to get the sleeve?" Her reflections were not coming from a caring compassionate place, it sounded more like she didn't want me to be small or healthy.

I said, "I was over 100 pounds overweight, not ten or 30. I was borderline diabetic, and I needed to have a complete change in my life so I can live not just for me but for my children." I explained that I didn't want to be the fat, out of shape parent who couldn't run, play, or get on amusement park rides with my children. "Plus," I told her, "I want to look damn amazing in my clothes and hopefully have great sex being healthier."

To be honest, it is possible that if she would have brought this up before my surgery, I may have reconsidered having it. Maybe I would have worked harder with my trainer, or I would have asked him to elevate my workouts to shock my body. Shit, to this day, I don't know why she changed. She never invited me to work out with her, but she invited our mutual friend who was bigger than her to make herself feel empowered.

MILESTONES

New body and a new attitude was exciting. We're about to celebrate our milestone ten-year wedding anniversary in 2016. But there was a situation that caused me great concern. In the back of my mind was the time in 2014 that J left his phone at home. I was nosy and I went through it. I stumbled upon a flirty conversation between him and another man whom I found out was a minister, in his text messages. The guy asked, "When did you know you were into men?"

My ex-husband stated, "I had my first experience in college." I felt my blood boiling. I couldn't believe everything he was saying to this man. I saw a video of the man preaching. In another text J said, "I always had a thing for ministers."

I thought, "I'm not a damn minister. What the hell is going on here?" I remember jumping off the bed with his phone pacing back and forth. I couldn't believe what I was reading. I called the guy he was texting, and I said, "How can you be a minister talking to a married man like this? What the fuck is wrong with you?" The man was silent. I guess he couldn't believe I was the wife of a man he was trying to seduce.

When J got home from work, he came into the bedroom looking for his phone. As he walked into the room, I held up the phone and asked, "What is this? Who is this man?"

J took the phone and said, "Nobody."

I was pissed. "I just called him," I said "He didn't say the same. I asked him if he is gay. Do you want to be with a man?"

J looked me straight in the eyes and said, "I love you and our family. I don't want to lose you." He never answered my question. That evening, I called off work because I couldn't focus on anything but replaying the text messages and conversation with J. I felt disappointed, and alone, even though I knew this man loved me. His actions told another story.

If he would have told me that he was interested in men, I would have stayed in California, never have moved to Georgia, and you would not be reading this book. When J stated that he loves me and his family I was apprehensive, yet I wanted assurance that he was not using me as a cover to mislead people into thinking he was straight.

I started to realize years later in my moments of reflection that my marriage was over from the time J started to look at men and compliment them in front of me. We had not been physically intimate for months. We had been sleeping in the same bed under different sheets. J was already checked out of our marriage mentally, emotionally, and physically before he made his announcement. It was clear that he didn't want me. I felt knowing that I'm married to a man that is supposed to love and protect me is no more. I was sleeping next to a stranger. I was completely alone.

I was apprehensive, confused and hoping that I was enough for him. As we danced in each other's arms at our anniversary celebration in front of our friends and family I hoped to God that J was being authentic. When I looked at him and watched him with our children, everything that I doubted melted away. I was prayerful that when he looked at me that he loved me as much as I loved him. I chose a beautiful cream lace dress to accent the curves of my new body, as I prayed that his passion was real, and not for show.

Even though no marriage is perfect, I can honestly say I was truly happy with my marriage. I loved J, with every part of my being, even when I doubted that he did not love and enjoy me. I dismissed those thoughts; I wanted it to be "happily ever after." All I saw was he and I, because if he wasn't happy, I expected him to let me know, he never communicated with me. Being married is hard, but we made it work.

Looking back, I truly believe that J did love me. He stayed in the marriage, and we built a life together. We had three beautiful kids and we worked with each other to make our dreams and aspirations a reality. At least J did. He must have thought I was taking too long to achieve my goals because I remember him saying one day, "If I would have waited for you to finish nursing school, I wouldn't have accomplished half of what I did."

That was hurtful. I started to calculate the things that I did for him and our family. I worked longer hours; I sat in the school carpool line for pick up and drop off; I handled most of the responsibilities with the children; I planned doctor's appointments; took them to recitals; took them to Girl Scout meetings and I was a troop leader. I went to community meetings in between my work and school schedules.

Even though I tried to explain, J did not understand that my race was different from his race. I was working toward my goal of becoming a nurse, my pace was just gradual. I couldn't rush my goals and balance the responsibilities I had as a mom and as his wife.

I don't think J ever thought I was going to finish my race.

"I had to sacrifice myself again."

~Erica Estella

TRANSITIONS

2017 was a year of transition for our family. My third pregnancy was more difficult than my two previous ones. I was considered a high-risk, geriatric pregnancy because of my age and uterine fibroids. The fibroids caused me to bleed at fifteen weeks.

High Risk Pregnancy

I remember waking up to light pink fluid coming from between my legs. I was scared and cried out to J. We jumped up, got the kids ready and went to the Emergency Room (ER). In the car I kept my legs clasped together because I didn't want any more fluid or even the fetus to come out of me. The urge to urinate was so strong, but I refused to give in because I didn't want to lose our baby.

On the way to the hospital, I emailed my doctor. When we arrived at the ER, I was immediately rushed to the observation room and that scared me. When the doctor came in to observe me, he was emotionless when he said, "You are going to have a miscarriage."

I started to cry uncontrollably. When he checked my cervix, it was still intact so he ordered an ultrasound to check the baby.

As I waited for my ultrasound I had a conversation with God. "This child that I'm carrying belongs to You, Lord. I'm just the vessel bringing forth Your creation." I prayed, "Have Your way, Lord." Then I stopped worrying.

When the ultrasound technician called me for the ultrasound my body was weak. When I laid down on the procedure table, I took a deep breath because I didn't know what to expect. It was like I was giving up, even after my prayer. I wondered, "Will I hear a heartbeat or not?" I could feel my heart pulsating faster than normal. When the technician found the fetus, she started measuring, but we could not hear the heartbeat of my unborn child.

For the second phase of the ultrasound, the technician assisted me to the restroom to empty my bladder. I didn't want to go to the bathroom because I was scared that I would lose the baby. I couldn't hold it, urine gushed out of me even though I tried to tighten my muscles. After I relieved myself, I looked at the toilet and saw bright red blood in the toilet. I knew it wasn't good, so I started crying.

I notified the tech about the blood and like the doctor, she was unfazed when she said. "Okay." She proceeded with the ultrasound, pressing onto my lower abdomen. I felt blood spurt out and my faith was depleted from my body. I couldn't believe that it was a possibility that I was losing my baby, but when the tech said, "Oh, let me get the fetus' heart rate!" I knew I had an on-time God in that moment. My soul and spirit were quickly revived. Joy started to return to me, I was so happy to learn that she found the heartbeat of my unborn child.

The test of my faith, going through that dramatic experience changed me mentally, emotionally, and spiritually. That day I surrendered everything to God: my pain, my broken relationships, my worries, and my heartbreak. That experience taught me that I am not in control of my life, or any life that grew within me, God is. I became extremely appreciative for every moment of every day, and I vowed not to waste my days on things that do not elevate me to my full potential.

After the ultrasound they took me back to my triage room. When my sister came into the room I started to cry. I grabbed her and held on tightly because I needed someone to be there for me in case I received more bad news from the medical team.

I didn't know Cheyenne had made it to the hospital so quickly. If you know my sister, her ass is late for everything, but she was right on time for me.

We waited for an obstetrician who was referred by my primary doctor. When the doctor walked in my room, her spirit was calming. She was a soft spoken, petite Indian woman. The doctor asked me a few questions and said, "The baby is fine."

J walked in the room as she said, "You need to take this pregnancy seriously." He listened to the doctor and waited until she finished to ask a few questions. I glared at him in surprise because all morning he seemed to be unaffected by what was going on with me. I noticed his bloodshot eyes and realized he had either been crying or praying hard for our unborn child and myself.

The doctor explained that my fibroid tumors were the cause of my bleeding. "You are in a high-risk pregnancy. I need to restrict your activities until the baby comes." The doctor restricted my activities to just walking, I couldn't have sex. "Well damn," I thought to myself, "I am already horny and in a sex drought. We don't even have sex regularly. Shit, what's new?"

I had to sacrifice myself again. Having a healthy pregnancy and birthing my son was more important than sex or working out. I wanted to bring forth this life within me.

Dr. J

The year that J earned his Doctorate in Public Administration, many possibilities opened for us and our family. Watching him defend his thesis made me proud and fascinated at the same time. Our mindset was "When I win, he wins, when he wins, I win," we genuinely had love for each other. Throughout our relationship we encouraged each other to be our best and reach for the sky. We were growing into ourselves as mature adults in our mid-thirties.

We planned his graduation party while J looked for a job. One evening as he was applying for jobs, J asked me, "Would you be open to moving?"

I was like, "Really? Where?" I was open to growing and adapting to a new state or city, which always had the best potential and would give him the dream job he worked so hard to achieve. When J mentioned D.C. and Maryland, I questioned, "Really? It snows out there, that's a huge difference in the weather. "

J continued searching for a job and to my surprise he asked, "What about Atlanta?"

"That seems cool," I said. "What do we have to lose? Let's pray on it and see how we feel in the morning." The next morning, I woke up and prayed about it. I remember telling J, "Apply for the job you're seeking in Atlanta." I didn't know that decision would mean I'd be losing my husband to a world I knew nothing about.

Considering a Move

With our family leaving California to pursue J's dream job, it meant I was sacrificing my career, family, and friends. We walked out of our comfort zone, into unknown territory and started to depend on each other for moral, spiritual, professional growth in this new transition of our lives.

I was ready to explore a new life in the South. I wanted to tackle new obstacles and be open to the possibilities of culture, food, and diversity. The South is mostly conservative. J and I have liberal beliefs, so moving to Georgia, a red state, meant I had to adjust quickly.

When J received the job offer, our lives started to move 100 miles per minute. We had to make the decision to sell our home or lease it. We decided to put our home on the market.

The day that J was leaving us to prepare the way in Atlanta, we looked at each other and he said, "We can change our mind."

I said, "We got this." I watched him leave out of our front door and get into his ride to the airport. It would be the last time he walked through the doors of our home. After I watched the car drive away, I turned to the boxes and blow-up bed in the living room. My heart was beating through my chest, and I had to sit down before I had a panic attack. To calm myself I started taking deep breaths. "I have to be the wife, mother, daughter, and employee during this process." I said to myself. "I have to arrange movers, assist J with finding an apartment to accommodate all of us and I have to make sure the kids are ready for the move."

With J gone, I was lonely and a little scared, but I didn't have time for doubt. Thank God that my mom was always there when I needed her. She really did not get to enjoy her retirement as planned due to my dad's health drastically declining after she retired. My dad's illness didn't stop my parents from showing up for their kids and teaching us life lessons that love does conquer all, or does it?

The day before my family took a plane to Georgia, my kids and I spent a few hours with my parents. My niece Monnie was there, too. I could see the sadness, love and hope in my parents' eyes because we were leaving. I took pictures of the kids with my parents to mark the moment.

When we were leaving emotions were high. My dad said, "See you later." My mom couldn't hold or kiss me, and my niece started to cry. I hurried to leave the house with quick hugs and kisses so my kids wouldn't start crying.

HELLO, GEORGIA

On October 14, 2018, our lives changed with the transition to Georgia. J flew into Los Angeles so we could all fly as a family to our new beginning. When we finally sat down on the airplane, I remember looking at J, and asking, "Is it really happening? We are really stepping out on faith, and I wouldn't do it with anyone else but you."

We moved during a pivotal election year. Stacy Abrams was the first African American Democrat running for the office of Governor in Georgia. I was ready to cast my vote in that election.

The Presidential election was important to my household, the United States, shit, the entire world. In Georgia we needed two Senate seats so the Democrats could have the upper hand and turn the state blue. That had not happened for over twenty-five years. For the first time ever, I went canvassing for the election to encourage people to rock the vote. I was excited, I wanted to see positive change come out of this election, especially a new president.

J enjoyed his new job with the County. I loved watching him in action. J's elevation had finally arrived, and I was elated. When he worked, he had a different walk and a different talk. He had achieved something amazing, and I felt so appreciative of him and his hard work and determination.

After a few weeks, Georgia started to feel like home. We explored our new city and loved the atmosphere, from the vibrant energy and plentiful, beautiful trees that surrounded our state. Watching my family in our new state, I felt warmth, a peace and an overwhelming gratitude. I thanked God for everything He had done for us.

We did not have the spirit of fear and we were learning more about ourselves. Our children were adjusting to their new schools, and my son, Jr and I enjoyed decorating, and cooking at home.

I was giving J and our children so much that I didn't have any life left to give myself after the day was done. Just thinking about my husband, I would get hot and wet, but I always made excuses for him not wanting to be intimate with me. "He is working and providing for us," I would rationalize, "I don't want to stress him out or make him feel that I am unappreciative." I love and respect what my husband has done and continues to do for our family.

I used to assist J with elevating his work attire that changed little after moving to Atlanta. J developed a different way of doing things and I was okay with that because in life it's about constantly changing and evolving into a better you. Things I would have questioned I didn't anymore. I had to trust and believe that he loved me, wanted us to grow and had great intentions. We were in this marriage together and he was truly my helpmate, as I was his.

I used to fantasize about fucking him despite seeing him every day. We were not sexually active. Honestly, I was oblivious to the situation. I started to think that I was not attractive to him anymore, or that I wasn't what he wanted. The drought in Georgia wasn't the first drought in which I mentioned earlier in our marriage, but I stayed, constantly questioning myself, "When is enough, enough? Then I said to myself I can't have it all so what I have with J is good enough and I should just count my blessings. When can I be touched and appreciated? When will my husband look me into my eyes and feel the love and arousal, he felt the day we said, "I do?" Those feelings were depleting me as days went on.

New Church

I focused on my family even though I couldn't give myself to my husband. J and I usually hosted Halloween parties for our family and friends with costumes and candy for the kids. In the H-team house we love Halloween. Since we had moved to Georgia, we weren't having a party, but we wanted to make sure our children enjoyed a trick or treat night somewhere that was fun and safe. J and the girls found a Trunk-Or-Treat event hosted by a church in our new city. When we pulled up, cars were lined up with candy and treats and there was a petting zoo onsite.

After that event, we started visiting the church and we joined after about a year. I was happy to have found a church home with everything we were looking for including a community that made us feel welcome and loved. The members became our new church family. They kept us busy. J was in the choir and worked with the men' ministry. I joined with marriage bible study, women and youth ministries and activities. I was busy with obligations at church and for the children. Life was lifing here in Georgia, we didn't miss a beat since the move.

My Parents Visit (2018)

We were adjusting to our new life and flowing into our new normal. My parents came to visit us in 2018 for the first time. I prepared for their visit and made sure we had enough food so my mom could cook all the Belizean food possible so we could have a taste of home. I was excited and emotional having my parents see us in our new element meant so much to me because we are continuously growing and learning about life around us. Seeing my parents would bring me so much peace.

I expected the summer 0f 2019 to be great, but I decided to visit California to assist with my dad because I knew my mom needed a break. She had recently retired and immediately began caring for my dad. When the kids finished school we flew out the next day. I took him to his dialysis appointments and other doctor's appointments. My dad was not in the best of health; he was on dialysis three times a week and had frequent hospital admissions. With all of the medical care he was receiving, he seemed to be getting weaker.

I cooked and helped him shower because he wasn't stable on his feet. I was so worried that he would fall and hurt himself. One evening, he stated,

"I can't believe it has come to this. You are my daughter, bathing me."

I said, "Dad you took care of me and all my siblings. It's our turn to take care of you. I love you daddy." I felt so sad for him. He wanted to keep his independence, he wanted to be active, travel, enjoy life with my mom and his family, but his body wouldn't allow him. My dad wasn't as robust of a man anymore, he was fragile and needed assistance around the clock.

Losing My Grandmother

Later the same year I returned back to California for the homegoing service of my maternal grandmother. She had been suffering from dementia for years. I did not like traveling for funerals, but I had to be at my grandmother's homegoing service. It was one that we all prepared for. As I communicated with my mom about my arrival, she mentioned my dad was in the hospital again. I was sad to hear that information about my dad.

It seemed that every week dad was in the hospital. My best friend Roshai picked me up from the Las Angeles airport and we had lunch before she drove to the hospital to see my dad. I walked into his hospital room and said, "Daddy, I'm back!" His cognitive response was delayed. He looked right through me as if he wasn't there. I had to walk closer to the bed and repeat who I was again, then he glanced at me and spit out some food that was in his mouth. I leaned over and kissed my daddy while holding back tears. It seemed that he worsened within weeks of me leaving in the summer. My daddy was declining mentally and physically. I was worried and scared. I needed to cherish these moments with him, and I needed to assist my mom with his aid.

As I was preparing for my grandmother's funeral my dad was in the hospital. I didn't think he would be able to attend the funeral. To our surprise, he checked himself out of the hospital against medical advice to support his wife—his best friend. My dad and my mom's bond was unbreakable even if it would cost him his life.

My dad walked into the church with his walker, trying to be strong for his wife, but it was too much on him. During the service, daddy started to feel so sick that he needed medical attention. After the funeral while everyone else proceeded to the cemetery, I stayed behind to call 911 so my dad would get back to the hospital.

As I was riding in the ambulance with him, I started preparing myself mentally to lose him. I had to come to terms with the fact that my daddy wasn't going to be here for as long as I imagined. I had to do my best to help my mom with whatever she needed me to do.

2019 RAIN

When I returned home, I spoke to J, about my parents moving in so I could give my assistance. My dad's health was declining and I needed to help my mom. It was amazing to have them with us, but seeing my dad declining was hard. He was in and out of the hospital even after moving to Georgia.

On New Year's Eve I went to the rehabilitation facility to pick him up to bring in the New Years of 2020, but he wasn't responsive. Dad had not touched his breakfast and it was 1:30 p.m. in the afternoon. From the rehabilitation facility, they rushed him to the hospital. For seven days, he was unresponsive, I could not hear his voice or talk to him. I was numb; it was like God was preparing me for the worst. 2020 had a rough start.

I had planned a trip to Hawaii for J's birthday, and I wanted to cancel it just to be with my parents. But my mom said, "Go. You both enjoy yourself. We'll be fine."

It was mind blowing touring the island of Waikiki, swimming in the ocean, eating amazing food at the

Lula and watching J dance on stage with the Lula girls. Between deep conversions and sightseeing, I kept thinking about what was happening with my dad. After returning from our trip to Hawaii, my family was doing okay, but my dad was declining.

On January 29, 2020, daddy took his last breath. He passed away with all his children and my mom around him. My daddy, my protector, was no longer with me. I felt alone. I didn't have anyone to console me besides my favorite cousin and small circle of friends. Yes, I was married, but my husband wasn't a person who knew how to console; he only knew how to be consoled.

When my dad died, it changed me. I didn't want to just live to live. I want to live and be happy. I started to count my blessings and not take anything for granted and I try to live each day with a driving purpose. I went through the year 2020 adjusting to being without my dad. Right after his funeral, the pandemic hit which put us all into a bubble.

While adjusting to our new normal of mask wearing and social distancing, I made sure we didn't catch "the C." I kept myself and my family safe from the virus that was killing so many people around the world. I felt like a robot following a clockwork schedule: getting up, being attentive to the children, feeding them, clothing them, bathing them and teaching them, day after day, after day.

I just wanted to get away from it all. I was suffocating from the death of my dad. I couldn't deal with it. I was dealing with the kids being solely dependent on me, with the kids being home with me 24 hours a day due to remote learning. I didn't have time to grieve. I could not reflect, think, cry, exercise, or scream, let alone sleep, I was on the clock with my family.

I had to put on armor and keep pushing. Their dad wasn't home and when he was, he was always working, preparing for elections. He was starting to work long hours and we only saw his shadow most days. I believe it made him happy when he wasn't around us. When he came home, I was exhausted, moody, and not interested in hearing about his day because he didn't care to ask about mine.

J would pull into our driveway and stay in his car talking on the phone for about an hour. I never thought anything of it, I had assumed he was speaking to his grandma, catching her up with his day or talking work stuff with colleagues. I was mentally and emotionally drained and didn't have the energy to ask him who he was talking to on the phone for hours. Maybe I didn't want to know. Plus, I didn't want him to feel like I was insecure about our relationship. How dare I say anything about him assisting with the kids when I was not contributing to the home financially.

After the U.S presidential elections, the Democrats won the White House and Georgia got the two senate seats. I was so damn happy, because I had heard from so many people that our vote doesn't count. Someone said we were wasting our time and that election showed me that democracy still exists, for now.

With things winding down with voting I was ready to start dating my husband again. I had missed him. I wanted my best friend to see me and appreciate us. I wanted to spend quality time together laughing, and talking about people we know. J was my comfort place and I wanted to grow old with him, having adventures to tell our children and future grandchildren.

Being with J and enjoying each other was something we should have done on a regular basis like we did when we were living back home. Making sure our marriage was great and that we were still happy with one another. It took for me to experience my father's death, the changes in my family, work, relationships, and now 2020 to feel the disconnect in my marriage.

2021

New year, new attitude.

The kids were finally back in school after COVID-19. J and I had a date planned so you know I was extremely happy because I was horny. "If he drinks, I could take advantage of him," I thought.

I got dressed in my favorite mustard yellow sweater, a pair of jeans, and some black boots. I met J at a local restaurant for dinner. I was ready to have alone time with my husband. We chose to sit on the patio because we wanted to keep a safe distance from others.

J ordered whiskey with an egg, and I had a refreshing mango margarita. After we received our drinks, there was an awkward silence. I broke it with a question I had asked several times before, "Why haven't we had sex?"

What J said shook me to my core. "I believe it's because I'm attracted to men."

I am attracted to men. These words clawed themselves into my heart and reverberated in me. "He invited me out for date night to tell me this shit?" I thought as I sipped my drink. "He finally told me the truth after 14 years of marriage. Damn!" I didn't know until that day that there was more to the story of him and his best friend. J told me that when he slept at his friend's house one night, he got an erection and pushed up towards him. I do not believe J's claim that nothing else happened.

I instantly became numb to everything around me walking, talking, working, and smiling. If someone would've stabbed me, I would not have felt it. I didn't know what to do with the deep pain I was feeling. This wasn't a phase he was going through; J was finally walking into his truth. I didn't want to be married to a gay man. I thought to myself, "How can I give him what he craves? Shit, he can't supply my cravings either."

I don't know how I held back tears from the betrayal at that moment. The words from his tongue killed every hope and desire I had for our marriage. I once thought our union was amazing and anointed by God, but it was just a foundation built on lies and deceit. I couldn't believe it took him all these years, three children and a move to Atlanta to have a fucking wakeup call!

The man sitting in front of me had vowed to protect me, love me, respect me, and honor us as a couple, but I didn't know him. He was selfish and lacked compassion. He did not think about his children or me. J was living for him now hopefully he can exhale now.

We had stood in a church in front of everyone we loved just to lie. "But he can't lie to God," I breathed through the flared nostrils. "Everything I did for this man!" I was holding back all my emotions. "I gave up my life in California to transition to Georgia to support his dream! I was the encouraging wife who supported and prayed for him. I was his biggest fan during all his accomplishments."

My mind turned to my family and my children. I had so much to do to prepare for a potential displacement. I had become too comfortable in the 14 years of being this man's wife. I realized that I did not have anything in place to move on quickly or smoothly after his announcement. He wanted to be with a man, something I was not.

I wish he had been honest from the beginning about his sexuality. If he had been honest with me, I would have least had an option to leave or stay, but I felt like he had trapped me. I didn't have a steady job after moving to Atlanta. I depended solely on him for financial support. I needed a way to revive myself and understand I would be emotional, but I had to push through for myself, and for my children.

I never thought that my high school sweetheart, the love of my life, would show me that I wasn't an option for him. It never crossed my mind that there would come a time in my relationship with J that he would ever be completely done with me. I wasn't expecting this announcement, but he had been struggling with who he really was and the life he had been living for way too long. J's honesty let me know that he needed to be free from me and from us. It honestly broke my heart into many small fragments.

My legs were shaking from the shock of this man's truth. I needed to express myself, but I couldn't do that in a restaurant full of white people. I was suffocating and couldn't catch my breath. I held back my emotions because I did not want to get irate in public, especially the South where they shoot and ask questions later.

I asked myself, "Did he really love and desire me? Did he really want this marriage or was he settling? Was he living the life he fully desired and wanted?" I couldn't stop thinking all the years we shared. Everything we built together was a façade. At that moment, I did not think I could ever give my all to another person, ever again.

Broken

You don't care about me
But I care about you
You don't love me
But I love you
You don't want me
But I want you
You broke me with your words
But I smile like I'm happy
You broke my heart
But you will never break me

- Erica Estella

The Aftermath

A few days after J's announcement, I moved into the guest room of our house. I needed somewhere to think so I could understand my new normal. I was feeling abandoned, empty, embarrassed, and alone. I didn't tell anyone about J's announcement because I was trying to protect him from judgment while I was yet again putting myself last. I did not want anyone questioning me, "Why didn't you know?" Or asking, "Did you know?"

No. I did not know that I was married to a man who was incapable of loving me fully. I did not know that I was married to someone that I could not give what he had a thirst for... We didn't kiss, hug or sleep in the same bedroom for months. My mind was racing,

I needed to know why, I needed to know where we would go from there, I needed to know why this happened. I pondered, "Was I that blinded to not see the signs right in my face or did I just turn a blind eye?"

Honestly, I did not know that J was gay. I could not comprehend that my ex-husband did not love me. He was always there for me as a supportive partner, he loved my family like it was his own.

Most women who have been hurt tend to blame themselves for what happened in their marriages. They try to retrace the red flags that were there from the beginning to escape the agony of heartbreak. I know that I agonized over what I could have been better in our marriage.

I thought about one Sunday when J and I were living in California. During service he had breakdown, or some may call it "he experienced the move of the Holy Spirit." Looking back, I believe that J was being convicted by God for his actions of deceit. He did all that dancing, looking as if he was being delivered, but he continued moving forward without acknowledging that he was a gay man pretending to be a loving, husband and father.

Lies

Why Lie
Why Lie
Why kill me with false words
Words that can poison the spirit
Spirit that decays bones
Why Lie, Why Lie

- Erica Estella

There were several incidents in my marriage that made me question J and his love for me. I remember that we visited a church service in a park one Sunday. I hoped we would have a date night after church, but J had other plans. As we got into the car he said, "I have a dinner date with someone from the church." He was referring to a man I saw at church, whom I believe was sweet to the touch, but I wasn't sure. He said, "I am taking you home."
It made no sense why J would dismiss me to take that man to dinner, but I let him drop me off at his mom's house. I waited a few minutes before I called him saying things that were not pleasant. Hearing his voice, my anger turns to fury. Shit, I wish I could remember what I said.

After I hung up on J, I called my best friend, Ro and told her what was going on. "I am feeling lonely and rejected." As soon as she could get there, Ro came over. A little after she pulled up, J came in right behind her screaming, "COME ON, YOU WANT TO GO EAT, LET'S GO!"

I didn't know how to respond to his tone. I gathered my things and got in the car leaving Ro standing outside looking confused. I watched Ro, as we drove away. J and I rode in silence until we reached the restaurant. I asked him, "What was so important for you and that boy to have dinner together? You know I wanted to spend today with you because we had busy weekdays."

All he said was, "We're here having dinner so let's eat." We ate.

Why did I stay for so long when I realized that the man I married was a liar? Or that he couldn't love, protect, nor did he desire me? How can someone lay with a woman, have children with her and just walk away? I became accustomed to unhappiness, lack of emotion and the sexless existence of my marriage. I had invested many years of happiness and peace.

Together, Yet Separated

J and I lived under the same roof and honestly, it was peaceful. Shit, we really didn't speak to each other. I felt that we needed to show our children that we loved them and that they were our focal point in this now broken marriage moving forward.

I bargained with God to give me back my husband's love so he would desire me and love me. I reminisced over 20 years of memories that turned into a nightmare. Bargaining was a waste of damn time because of the lies, neglect, and blunt disrespect from the heartless human I was married to.

I put my all in our marriage and gave up so much to give this man the world. My plan for my life is not always what God wanted for me. I fell and it redirected my mind, I lost everything to rebuild and grow on my own. I know God didn't want me to be in a lonely, sexless marriage. I was ready to release my union so I could be free of death and learn to love myself again. I wanted to grow and walk forward in my refined life.

The Breaking

J and I continued to live in separate bedrooms, barely speaking to each other. Thankfully, my girlfriend Brit, was staying with us. She had relocated to Georgia from California and was staying with us until she found her own place.

One morning Brit and I went to get breakfast at the Breakfast House for the family. I just needed to get out of the house because the energy in the home was heavy and suffocating. I left the house wearing burgundy tights, brown snow boots and a green and pink sweater. I looked like a mess!

I sat at the counter looking at the menu and my eyes wandered toward the cook. I noticed his nice-looking ass. I didn't know what was going on in me, or what I needed to get in me, but I enjoyed the feeling of admiring a man from afar. He must have sensed me looking at him because he turned around and our eyes connected. I hurried to look away and pretended to focus on the menu. Eventually my eyes gravitate back to that delicious man.

After I placed my order the cook turned around and made the hand gesture of a phone. In my mind I was like, "Baby you can have it and me as well."

I carried the food back to the car and told Brit what happened. She said, "What? You did what?"

I repeated myself as I drove away, "I gave him my number." I truly felt myself for that moment. I knew my life wouldn't be where I needed it to be until I figured out my next move in the marriage.

When I pulled into the driveway I saw J with yellow roses in his hand. It was for Valentine's Day. I knew J wasn't going to do anything for me because he really didn't like to celebrate. It shocked me to see him with those roses. He called commercial holidays like that "overrated."

Brit and I looked at each other like, "what the hell?" I got out of the car and when I went into the house, I looked closely at the yellow roses. I appreciated his kind gesture, but the roses weren't fresh. They were not really yellow, and they did not even have a fragrance. "He must have gotten them from the discount area at the market," I thought. Those roses were a few days old and wilting. It made me feel even worse that J was still trying to have a make-believe marriage after he told me he was gay.

All that Valentine's Day, I could not stop thinking about the guy I met at the Breakfast House. I wanted to get to know him, I wanted to feel something other than sadness and rejection. I wanted to feel wanted, and desired. I was a lost child in this world without protection. My dad was gone, and my husband did not want me. I felt myself gravitating to a strange man who showed an inkling of attention. J had made me insecure to the point that I thought I needed a man to approve my worth.

I couldn't decay. I needed to truly find my purpose through all the mess I was facing. It wasn't easy to give it to God, but I had to. I was so damn mad and hurt. I wanted to hurt J the way he hurt me and I wanted revenge, but it wasn't in me to hurt him. How could I hurt someone I still loved.

Even though I wanted to keep protecting him, I couldn't be his security blanket any longer. I had to surrender my pain to God because it was going to kill me emotionally and physically.

My Backbone

My family is everything to me and despite having family living with me throughout my divorce process, I still felt disconnected from everyone. My mother is my best friend, but she didn't know what was going on. I wanted to tell her everything, but it wasn't the time or place. One thing about my mom is that she doesn't like seeing her children hurt, no mother does. I didn't want to weigh her down with my situation especially after losing her mother, my dad, and her brother.

When I finally told her about separating from J, she was extremely hurt. Our conversation was intense, and she said, "He is still my son and I love him." My mom never stopped loving J; she always spoke highly of him because she didn't want to interfere in our relationship. She wanted us to handle things like mature adults—without outside influences, including her.

I spoke through tears, "Mom, I understand, but I need you to protect me like his mom is protecting him. He hurt me mommy. He doesn't care about me, or our children. He was just pretending to love me. He always wanted us to look a certain way for church folks and social media, but deep down in the roots of things he knew that he could never be fulfilled to love me and give me all of him."

My mom and my cousin Andrea were the only two people who saw me cry during that time. She watched me stay in bed because I was too emotional to care for my children. She cooked, cleaned and assisted me when I couldn't do anything for myself.

I was tired of being ashamed of my marriage ending. I was just so damn tired of not holding J responsible for his actions and lack of emotions pertaining to me, our marriage and our children. After J moved out, our divorce was soon to be finalized.

I looked at him differently when he asked if I could start paying him to take my mom home because as he stated, "It's going out of my way."

When he told me that my seventy-year-old mom, who takes care of his kids, could catch a ride share to his house, I was shocked. He wanted me to send a car to her house and drop her off at his place so he could drive her to my house when he brought the kids home on every 2, 4 and 5th Sunday. I didn't want to argue with him so when he sent me the screenshot of the cost of the ride I sent the funds immediately. I understand that people tend to show their true colors when money is involved, when they feel you're not showing them empathy, and when they can't control the narrative.

I didn't tell my mom he made that statement because I wanted to keep the peace between them. I wanted to make sure she was able to keep seeing him as her son. I let mom know that a ride share would be taking her to my ex-husband's house. She read the message but didn't respond. That Sunday evening when he brought the girls and my mom home, I assumed that the ride went smoothly when she didn't mention anything about it. Taking her home Friday after she spent the week, I asked her about the ride.

To my surprise, he had picked her up even though I sent him money. He never communicated that he changed the plan or even said he would reimburse me. I dismissed the situation all together, I didn't want to entertain any more negativity. My mother had made up her mind that she would no longer ride in his car. She had known him for most of his life. It hurt her that he had me pay him to transport her home after she watched, cooked, cleaned and washed our children's clothes.

I don't know what my mother said to him that day. She said her peace and that was that.

TRUE COLORS

I told my therapist about J and she asked, "Why couldn't he come out earlier? Why wasn't he honest? The evidence was right there." She said, "J must have been trying his best to be released from you so he could be his authentic self, but he lied several times to remain in his comfort zone."

I started to look at my choices and why I didn't listen to my intuition. I was trying to be strong enough for both of us and just walk away so he could truly love himself instead of lingering in a marriage that wasn't pleasing to him sexually, emotionally, or physically.

I was still hoping after all he said to me that our relationship would get better, I don't think he understood what we had was worth fighting for. I remember asking him about celebrating our 15th anniversary. He said, "Yes, we can both have dates on our anniversary." That made me sick to my stomach to have this man say those words. The words from his tongue were killing me, but I never let him see me cry.

"He will never see me broken because I'm not," I vowed to myself."

That made me call the guy from the restaurant. I wanted to be held and seen by someone who wanted me. It didn't matter if it was for one night, I just wanted to be touched. Ironically, I chose to meet the cook for breakfast. We enjoyed the first date and started doing other things together such as hiking and dancing.

Rodriquez made me nervous. I had never dated a thug before, but it was exciting. I couldn't resist him at all, especially when he looked at me as if I was the only person in the world. I know we hung out for only a short time, but it seems as if he was here to revive me, make me feel secure again and bring feeling back to my numb existence.

Rodriquez was sent to help me realize that divorcing my gay husband had nothing to do with me, or how other men perceive me. He confirmed that I am wanted, desired, and admired. I enjoyed being held. I knew I wasn't going to marry Rodriquez, but for the months we were together, he loved me and I felt safe with him. He provided more affection than my husband of 15 years did. We got close quickly and he swept me off my feet.

I didn't know what I was feeling, I didn't know if it was reality, but it was just a dream, I didn't want to wake up. I wanted to get lost in his world and indulge all my senses in him. He wanted all of me.

I didn't want anything serious with Rodriquez because I wasn't fully healed from the hurt in my marriage. Rodriquez was my drug. I just needed a fix from him. He made me feel high on sex like I never felt before. I appreciate him because he came into my life when I thought I wasn't attractive or that I needed validation of my worth.

My feelings for my husband started to fade from my mind, body, and soul. The connection I thought we would have for a lifetime was gone and he was no longer desirable to me. I didn't hope to be with him again, I didn't miss his touch, his conversation, or his smell. You can't make someone love you unconditionally especially when they are broken and don't love themselves. I came to that realization after months of separation.

I was choosing not to be a wife who settled for less than God's best. I wasn't going to stay married because of children or the beautiful comfortable lifestyle that we created. He couldn't give me any of the things I desired, and I wasn't going to deprive myself any longer to make him happy. I refused to keep his secret in the closet while I was dying spiritually in public.

"Some days were harder than other days, but I'm a warrior."

OPEN AND CLOSED

At one time I had told my ex-husband, "I will not divorce you. We can be the new "Modern Day Family." I had considered staying married in an open marriage for my children's security. I wanted the best for them and that meant I had to sacrifice my happiness and desires for them.

J had stated, "I'm not going to leave until the kids get older." He wanted me to live alone for another 15 – 20 years until our children were grown and I was old with nobody to love me. He wanted me all to himself while he tasted the flavors of Atlanta. That was not happening!

We were all in for an open marriage until J told me he had been intimate with my only sister's live-in boyfriend and a close friend's husband. I started to feel the damn walls closing in on me. I quickly removed myself from him before I lost it. His admission had taken away everything from me in one night. Yet, he still wanted to control the entire situation that his lies created! Some may say, "He did love you? Did he? That's a question I will ask him one day.

J was being reckless with his actions and especially with his words. After learning about his infidelity, I needed to escape and that's what I did. Right into someone else's arms for healing and comfort. I was lusting for Rodriquez.

Going Back to Cali

In January of 2021 the family was heading to Los Angeles for his grandma's 80th birthday celebration. J had purchased the tickets months in advance of his life-changing announcement on January 7. Although we were not in a good place, I wanted to go to the party because I love his entire family and it was important for my children to celebrate the life of their great grandmother.

Our relationship was deep, especially because of our children and the fact that our families were so intertwined with each other. The end of our marriage showed me that it did not matter about being related, it was the principle of knowing I was lied to and deceived for so long that mattered.

A few days before our trip, I recall hearing a phone conversation between J and his mom. Before they ended the call he said, "See mom we are still close. We're best friends." That shit didn't sit right with me.

I called a close friend and told her that we were coming to LA. I asked if I could stay with her while I was there. She was excited and opened her doors for me. I was so happy that I didn't have to fake a happy marriage to a man who didn't care about how he was hurting me or the bridges he was shattering on this road of finding himself as a gay man.

We landed in LA and his mom picked us up. I was so happy to see her and the rest of the family. When we arrived at her house and she started to remove the luggage from the car, I told her, "You can leave mine outside, I'm staying with Mrs. B, this trip." My mother in love look at me with sadness and confusion. I didn't know what to tell her, but I hoped her son would take advantage of their days together to enlighten her with the truth and nothing but the truth.

Mrs. B came to get me and I caught her up on everything that was going on. My cousin Andrea came over and we all enjoyed each other's company. My girlfriends wanted to hangout every night I was there because it was also close to my birthday. I loved being with them all. I wanted to get away from it all and live, smile and laugh my ass off on this trip. I did just that, going out with my girlfriends, cousin and just enjoying this moment of normalcy.

We were sharing life stories and I felt vulnerable. I truly appreciated that space because I remember my therapist saying, "Vulnerability is a sign of strength not weakness. It's helping you heal from the inside out." That day I was so vulnerable all I could remember was tears and snot running down my face like the river. Putting my heart on the table I felt so light after that genuine experience.

Bad News

While enjoying my family and friends I called to make sure Rodriguez was doing well. He was somewhat in his feelings when I was leaving. I guess he thought I would meet and be with someone else. Honestly, I needed to be by myself, to learn myself and my true purpose. I didn't have time for what he was thinking about. I kept the peace by calling him every day on facetime.

My friends and family surprised me with a pre birthday party with a male stripper. We danced, laughed, cried, ate good food and enjoyed every moment of our time. In the back of my mind, I was feeling broken and defeated, but being there and seeing people who truly loved, and supported was reviving me back to life.

When things started to slow down after the party we went to a hotel. My friend had booked a room for us to stay up and talk all night. Before getting too comfortable, I called Rodriquez to make sure he was home after work. I wanted to hear his voice and check in about our day. Instead of seeing and hearing him over the video chat, I was speaking to a stranger that had answered his phone.

I was shocked at first. I asked the man, "Where is Rodriquez?" As I was waiting for his response, I was looking at his face taking a mental picture in case I needed to identify him in a line up. The man stated, "They are working on him." That's when I noticed the flashing paramedic lights and I heard myself yell, "What do you mean working on him?"

"He was shot." I heard the man on the phone say, "... unresponsive."

I was confused. "What's wrong? What happened? Who was driving? Why aren't you shot?" All I remember was falling to the floor in disbelief. I couldn't take the pain.

I couldn't believe that Rodriquez was gone. He promised me that he wouldn't leave me, and he did! I was numb, I couldn't believe death had hit me four times in less than a year: my dad, my uncle, my marriage, and now Rodriquez. I had to ask myself,

"What is going on?" So many things were happening at one time, I was overwhelmed.

I didn't think I could live anymore after the news of Rodriguez's' passing. I was still mourning my dad's death. All the men who loved me were gone. The one who hurt me willingly and deliberately was still alive. "Why!!!!" I cried out.

My sister, cousin and friends had to console me all night. Not long after I finally fell asleep, I was awakened by a phone call from a detective. The detective knew my name and where I lived. Shit, I was surprised he didn't read me my credit score. The detective asked about the last time I spoke to Rodriquez. The whole thing made me feel like I was a suspect in the man's murder, and I was over 2,000 miles away in Los Angeles. I answered all the questions then ended the call.

I wanted to isolate myself, roll up in a dark corner and stay there. I only wanted to mourn. My cousin told me, "Everything happens for a reason," you could have been there and be dead as well it wasn't your time Erica." After that conversation I had to snap the hell out of the grieving mood I had been holding inside since the passing of my daddy.

I had to survive, be proactive and live and stay strong for my children. They are the most important things to me; they are my lifeline. I prayed harder because of them. I worked harder because of them. I spoke life over myself even more because of them. I kept smiling and moving. Some days were harder than other days, but I'm a warrior. I felt like the world was going 100 miles per minute around me while I stayed at a standstill.

Celebrating Life

While we prepared to celebrate the 80th birthday of J's grandmother, I was trying to cope with everything happening in my life. I truly believe the old saying, "What doesn't kill you makes you stronger."

I was living the lesson that my life is not my own. God is the author and I'm the pages He is writing on. God has been guiding me my entire life. In those difficult moments, I was not listening to Him. Sadly, I had been trying to learn and grow on my own. It took all the chaos I was living through at the time to change me.

On the day of the party, my first cousin Andrea and my friend Mrs. B went with me. When I walked in and got close to my husband, I thought he would move to the side so we could pass by him. To my surprise he stood up and gave me a hug. To me, that action was his public way of asking me to shelter him. He wanted people to see that we were good. For me to hug him in front of his family, we didn't have to explain anything to anyone about what was going on. All I could think about was how to protect myself and my children from this stranger who was holding me.

I was in total disbelief of how he could still pretend to love and protect me when he was totally doing the opposite behind closed doors. I let go of the embrace and sat down. It was a damn shame how he tried to play me. But, like a mature woman, I smiled and enjoyed the celebration. I greeted his family, took a few pictures with his GG, and I even assisted with slicing the cake.

When the event was over and we all prepared to leave, our children did not want me to leave without them. I think they could feel that something was different between J and I. T started to cry and she asked, "Mommy, can you stay?"

I remember looking at J's Auntie Sheena, and I was holding back tears. What was us—a normal, happy, beautiful family, was no more. Sheena couldn't say anything because I believe if she did, she would've started to cry uncontrollably. I quickly gave my kids a hug and proceeded to leave the party before I broke down. That was the first time it truly hit me that this was the new beginning of our unhappy ever after ending.

As we got in the car, we talked about how utterly shocked we were by J's attitude. I said to my out loud to myself, "The way he felt he needed to speak to me as if it was a pity party."

Aunt Sheena stated, "So sad." I couldn't understand why she would say that to me. What was "so sad," to her? Was it because our family dynamics had changed? Was it because he revealed his true sexual orientation to her? Or was it sad because the kids were now going to suffer the consequences of a broken home? Was it so sad that our marriage of 14 years was over?

I pondered those two words so much that I had to text J to ask what she meant. "Are you telling your family the truth, because if not, I will."

The text message he sent me in response must have been his alter ego. The words I was reading were not from the man who had embraced me tenderly at his GG's party a couple of hours earlier:

Whatever I am telling my family is the truth. You shouldn't communicate with me unless it's regarding the children or our household expenses. I will notify my lawyers in the process of getting a divorce.

I had no idea what he was talking about. "He is totally losing his mind," I thought. I told myself I didn't need his mess. I told my friends, "I need to get a lawyer, too." Then it hit me, I wasn't working, I didn't have steady income to help me fight him for what is rightfully mine. I started to get scared and nervous. It was an unfamiliar place for me to be dependent upon a man like that.

J did not want to let me go, and he did not want me at the same time. I could not live another 10, 15, or 20, more years in an unhappy marriage for the sake of our children. Marriage should be peaceful, growth, fulfilling, exciting, full of sex, and that simply wasn't happening for me. I wanted my husband to see me, but he couldn't because he was blinded by the dicks that he wished could be on the tip of his lips.

I started to cry. Mrs. B said, "Call the lawyer you found, and I'll pay your deposit. I need you to be free and happy." That is when I knew I had to accept this chapter of my life. to release J so I could truly move on and grow without him. Part of me wished I could have trusted my intuition and closed this chapter sooner than later. Life was going to be different for me. I would have to navigate this world alone after being a part of someone's life for over three decades. I was scared and worried about the unknown and what was expected of me. Why was I holding on to a fading dream?

Even though my marriage was over it did not mean I could stop living or that I would never find love again. I was stressed because I didn't know if I could make it, let alone survive with my children as their sole parent. This was my new chapter and I planned to move forward and explore even though I might fall or fail. I will continue to stride and push through all the obstacles I will face during my transition. I had to wake up and let go of my knight in shining armor. I deserved more than the glass house façade of a marriage.

Rodriquez's death was still hard for me. I was putting on a show, smiling with a strength that only came from God, to keep it normal for my kids while we were in Los Angeles. I made sure we took the kids to the beach. We had a blast making sandcastles, getting buried in the sand, and listening to the water smash shoreline. Everything was going great until I caught J, looking at someone in the distance. When he said, "Wow, they look good," at first, I thought he was looking at a Caucasian man stretching on the sandy beach. When I followed his eyes, I realized he was looking at two black, masculine men working out on the boardwalk. They were dripping with sweat and the sun glistened off their bodies.

All I could do was scowl at him with disgust. He was so damn disrespectful, yet comfortable to express his sexual orientation right in front of me. I believe he wanted to break me. He wanted to dehumanize me while he found himself; it must have made him feel empowered to see me alone and unwanted. I had to turn my head and smile to cover my broken heart as our children played in the sand.

I refocused on the moment with them, enjoying the beach. I took a deep breath, but I couldn't release the oxygen. I inhaled, but it was stuck in my throat like I was stuck in this dead marriage. I couldn't believe I had children with a man that deceived me. He couldn't love me; everything I believed we were, was a nightmare.

He made me leave my family, especially my dad, whose health was declining. He made me rip my children from their school, friends and family. I gave up my career in California. He could have left us there while he experimented with his new life and the fruit thereof.

Back to Reality

By the time we got back to Georgia, I was trying to avoid J at all costs. As long as he was out of my sight, he was out of my mind. Seeing his ass day and night and living with him for nearly a year since his announcement was coming to a damn boil.

I needed something to change quickly. I needed him to move out and move on to his new profound life. Even though I was tired of living with him, I never disrespected him unless I had to protect myself and my children.

There was an incident during my birthday weekend, and I wanted to go out, even if it was by myself. I wanted to get away. J told me that one of his friends was coming to visit LA and he was going to celebrate his birthday with him. I knew who it was. Yes, that person was also gay or zesty with a wife and a child.

J said, "I'll be at the hotel with my friends, and I won't be staying home this weekend, but I will bring them by the house."

I asked, "Who are they?" J never replied to me. So, when he got home that evening I asked him again, "Who is coming to the house besides your friend that I know?"

J responded, "I don't have to tell you anything because this is my house!"

All I remember is seeing red! I wanted to kick his ass, but I just said "OUR MONEY bought this house! How the hell can you fix your mouth to tell me that, when we didn't have a damn penny after we got married? We built this lifestyle together."

After our argument his friends came into the house and as they passed me in my kitchen not one of them said a word to me. They all must have known about our situation and were there to see if I was going to get out of line so he could have support if things got physical between us. But the God I serve was there that night. HE told me, "Get your keys and leave," and that's what I did.

I drove away with rage and hurt that hit me at once. Our children were at the house and J felt so bold to have those men over there who bluntly disrespected me by walking into our family home with my kids and could not speak to me, the woman of the house. That incident told me that he was speaking poorly of me and that they didn't respect me at all. Why would they respect me when my husband didn't? From that point I was completely done with J.

I didn't want anything to do with J because he was reckless and insensitive. I didn't trust him or the words that came out of his mouth. That day, J became my enemy, and I planned to move accordingly around him.

I didn't know where to go, but I had a song playing on repeat on my playlist called "Why Not Me," by Tasha Page Lockhart. The song gave me clarity and assurance that my trials and tribulations are not in vain. As I sang, I grew in victory. I needed to continue staying humble, being kind, walking in patience and having an understanding that God will use me for His glory.

I was in my feelings after hearing my gospel song. I ended up driving around the city of Roswell until I ended up at a tavern. I didn't order anything to eat, but I sure did drink a margarita on the rocks. I sipped my drink and watched the people who were enjoying life while I sat there trying not to cry.

I am far from perfect, and I did things in my marriage that I'm not proud of, but I would never have bluntly disrespected my husband the way he disrespected me. I had even encouraged my family and friends to respect him because he was the father of my kids. I can't say the same for his followers. His immature cousin attacked me on social media and some of his family gave me the cold shoulder after almost two decades of marriage. The division was real on his side, not mine.

Tired

Fuck, respect me
14 years of marriage, three children
You bring your side piece into our home
you desire a man after I given you all of me
Fuck, respect me as your wife, the mother of your
children. I'm tired of all this shit, I'm, tired of all of you

- Erica Estella

"I believe we were doing the best that we could as parents despite the circumstances of our divorce."

~Erica Estella

DIVORCE HURTS CHILDREN, TOO

I focused on my future and the future of my three children. I was concerned about their path of being emotionally and mentally healthy. I did not want them to have any negative outbursts due to the change in our family dynamics. Especially after J had a talk with them about his new life, without me being present. I know children are resilient, I just didn't want to think for a second that our children would be affected by this change.

Our children were hurting and I didn't always see it. The foundation of what they knew as a family was based on sinking sand. I was a Daddy's Girl and I considered him my first love. Because of the divorce, I did not want my daughters to look at their father and other men negatively, assuming they all lie. I wanted my son to see his father as a strong man.

I don't know if my children understood the divorce, I think they took it personally. I always tried to keep the communication open between us. J and I brought our daughters into my bedroom, a familiar and comfortable place for them. We wanted a haven to communicate about our marriage and that we were separating. "Your dad will be moving out," I told them. "I know you feel the difference in our relationship: J and I weren't sleeping together, we didn't go on dates, we didn't touch each other, we hardly spoke, and we were hardly alone in the same room for a long period of time. I wanted our children to understand that our relationship ending had nothing to do with them.

In the family meeting J told the girls he fell out of love with me. Internally I was raging because he forced me to fall out of love with him through his actions of watching other men around me, by complimenting their body and admiring them the way he never admired me.

Unfortunately, despite us telling them they were not the cause of our divorce, it seemed that they felt like they were the cause. We told our children that us being separated had nothing to do with them, but with him falling out of love with me.

To keep things as normal as possible when I did not have to work, I enjoyed spending quality time with my children. It was an adjustment to not have the support of a husband to assist me when I was exhausted. I had been home with my youngest child for the majority of his life, and I know not seeing me or his father every day might have caused confusion.

I believe we were doing the best that we could as parents despite the circumstances of our divorce.

Our children were processing the change from having two parents in the house and now not having access to their father, then we added the words, "divorce," and "your dad is gay," to the mixture. It must have been hard for them. Shit, it would be hard for anyone.

One of our daughters started to change. I recognized that she started to wear dark baggy clothes. She lost interest in things that she enjoyed and would only do them if I forced her to. She was becoming distant from me and everyone else in the family. She stayed in her room, only coming downstairs to eat and chat a little. I would always ask her about her day at school and she only spoke a few words at a time, "It's good," or "It was fine." She was no longer animated in her responses.

The situation with J really affected her emotionally, spiritually and physically. It pains me to say that my child started to hurt herself by cutting herself. I was in my own grief not knowing my child was trying to escape life all together. Our divorce shook up the most valuable and sacred relationship my children had seen because it was based on lies.

I was at work when a concerned school counselor called to talk to me about my child. She said, "I noticed your daughter's wrist and wanted to bring it to your attention that there are cuts up and down her upper arms." When she was talking, I remember the feeling of my heart sinking down to my feet. I didn't know how to react to the fact that my life was caving in, and it was swallowing my children, too. I didn't know how to react or who to turn to without them judging her or judging me as a parent. My child was crying out for help.

I had my own therapist and I leaned into my therapy heavily. I wanted to be mentally, spiritually, and emotionally stable for my children and myself. I used to cry with my therapist when I talked about the times I felt unworthy of love and so insecure that I tended to gravitate to any man who showed me the attention I was lacking. I don't know what was wrong with me or why I had to go through what I went through with J.

But the thing with children not living with both parents is that the part-time parent doesn't see or understand the child. I remember calling J about the incident and he said, "This situation only happens when she's in your care." I didn't call to be lectured, I wanted to inform him about our daughter and have a united front to make sure we got the proper therapy to assist us.

I was silent during his rampage because I didn't want to go the fuck off on him. I had the right to scream, "THIS IS ALL YOU, YOUR LIES, YOUR DECEIT, YOUR NEGLECT! You're hurting all of us and then you expect us to support and encourage your new life, get the hell out of here!" But I didn't.

I was already feeling bad as a parent. His anger was only going to fuel more of my own rage, so I listened to his blame. I didn't want to see my child hurting to the point that the only way to express herself was to injure herself. I needed her to be mentally and emotionally stable. I knew I had to do everything in my power to get her the help she needed.

Around Christmas in 2021, she asked, "Why do we celebrate Christmas? I wish we were still in LA, in our small house."

I stopped what I was doing to give her my full attention and asked, "Why? We live in a bigger house. You have your own room and bathroom."

"Mom," she said, "in LA we were always together, we were happy, we were a family." When she said those words, tears came to my eyes, but I couldn't cry, I had to be her strength as she wrapped her arms around me and cried uncontrollably. I couldn't say or do anything but hold her. I was thinking she was talking about the house or missing LA, but she was referring to us as a family. My daughter remembered all the times we were doing things together, from picking out our Christmas tree, decorating the house, hot coco and movie night just being silly, and loving each other.

I don't know if she was seeing and feeling the rejection of her father towards me and believing that is how a wife should be treated. What I knew is that I refused to allow my children to witness a cold and unloving marriage and then have the notion that is what marriage is all about.

Our second child is outspoken and doesn't hold anything back. When we sat with our children and told them that we were separating she was silent. T didn't quite understand what was going on. She asked a question like any child her age would have asked, "Do you guys love us?"

We both said, "Yes, we do."

I said, "Our relationship as husband and wife will change, but not our love as your parents will not. You all are our priority and that will never change."

Our oldest was the only child who asked for and was adamant about having a therapist. I told her and our second child, "If you want to speak to someone other than your dad and myself, I will schedule you both appointments for a therapist. I really had not seen changes in my second child. I made sure to spend time with her and reminded her, "Stay confident in who you are because you are loved."

I thought Jr. was too young to know what was going on, but he realized that mommy and daddy don't live together anymore. He really misses his dad and when it's his weekend he is always really thrilled about leaving. One day he asked, "Mommy, can you marry daddy?"

I said, "What, son?"

"Daddy broke up with his girlfriend, so you can marry him now." Out of the mouth of babies. If only he knew his daddy and I were already married and that his dad did not find me physically or sexually attractive. How could I tell my son that his father did not want me or any other woman.

I did not fail my children. I did not fail myself. Even when failure was knocking at my door, it was never an option for me. Failure tried to sneak in, tried to break down all the normalcy I had known for years. Our children realized that what they were accustomed to was over, but I chose not to fail them.

"The only way to conquer my brokenness was to give it to God."

~Erica Estella

THE WOMAN IN ME

What woman does not want to be desired, protected, and taken care of by their spouse? I didn't ask for much, just transparency. Being married I fell in and out of love with my husband due to life, raising a family, working, and not having time to fully be sexually intimate with him.

I admit going through the motions and making sure I kept up the illusion of being a happy wife because I was with a man who was respected in the community. But at the same time, I felt like I was dying emotionally, spiritually, and physically being in a marriage that wasn't fulfilling. The man had not been looking at me sexually, he did not compliment me, nor did he smile at me. I looked back at pictures that we've taken, and it was not always a genuine smile. It looks like he is forcing himself especially after the move to GA.

I didn't need validation from him, I know I look good, and I am confident, I just wanted to make sure J found me attractive and wanted me. When it was proven that he did not want me, I knew that I had to get myself together financially, physically, and most of all spiritually because my faith was tested.

I continued to maneuver into my new phase despite having days I just wanted to not get out of my bed and stay there. I remember being on my Paparazzi Live on Facebook for the entire month of April in 2021. It was crucial that I keep pressing forward. I was at my lowest point during the separation, but I kept smiling while I was selling my jewelry to keep the tears from flooding down my face.

I was showing supernatural strength and power which exhausted me mentally, emotionally and spiritually. I didn't have the tools to push through or the fight to move forward. The only way to conquer my brokenness was to give it to God. Strength came from John 10:10 which says:

The thief comes only to steal and kill and destroy; I have come that they may have life and have it too full."

This verse has kept my mind on Jesus, I know God didn't put me here to just abandon me. I wasn't ready to give up on life. I wanted to live, and I needed HIM to revive me.

I knew that I needed to get a job. J had stopped giving me money and I was using it for the kids. My Paparazzi jewelry business did not generate steady income to feed me and my children or to buy personal hygiene items. I started looking at hospitals and revising my resume, but I needed something quickly. I knew the process would be long for the hospital. I applied for a job at a local grocery store. The process moved so quickly that I had an interview on a Tuesday morning and started working Wednesday morning, just like that.

I was somewhat embarrassed to be working at the grocery store deli knowing my professional background, but I appreciated the opportunity that I was given. I have a different kind of respect for grocery store employees. Several times I found myself in the deep freezer getting the produce and I would cry. I would stand there crying with tears freezing on my face.

Working at the grocery store I was feeling hopeless and stuck, like my life was going backward instead of forward. I didn't have access to the things that I had become accustomed to like getting a simple pedicure and manicure or sitting in the chair to get my Sisterlocs retightened.

I was asking for money from my mom, and I had friends giving me money until I got back on my feet. I was scrambling for money, so I had to work a minimum wage job. I was making $15 an hour and it felt like God was punishing me for not fighting for a marriage that wasn't fighting for me.

I didn't like the damn hours, 4 a.m. to 11:00 a.m. I had to stand on my feet the entire shift preparing salads, sandwiches, wraps, pudding and platters. Cleaning was a non-stop part of the job, too. Even though I really enjoyed the job, I knew it was just a steppingstone to my new life in Georgia as a divorced woman.

I remember calling my mom on my first shift during my lunch break. I said, "Mom, I don't want to eat anything, I just want to sit down!" Sitting down was a luxury, a little thing I took for granted. I saw a chair in the breakroom. It was like I won the lotto! My feet were hurting, and my back was tight.

Throughout the weeks working at the grocery store, I was still updating my resume to get back in the hospital. I have a passion for helping people and I was ready to reestablish myself. I had not worked in the medical field for three years and I needed to review and practice cardiac rhythm skills, to be amazing at my job.

BETRAYAL

I became an American Heart Instructor for Basic Life Support and purchased my manikins as well as kept up with my certifications for the hospitals. I called former co-workers, friends, supervisors, and charge nurses. I had a mentor who is a Doctor of Nursing and I texted her to ask if she would be a reference for me. She gave me her email and we proceeded to catch up. I told her I was doing well, "Brighter days are ahead," I told her.

I mentioned that I was going through a divorce, and she responded , "I sensed it. I get prophetic interpretation," she said. I was shocked at her revelation because J and I were very private, I knew it was God who revealed any information to her. We don't display public drama or negativity of any kind on social media.

My mentor continued, "God is not the author of confusion. You should thank God for opening your eyes. Continue to pray for your husband because he is blinded. The spirit of incubus and succubus and homosexuality is trying to destroy homes and families." When she said those words, I was in shock.

I could not understand how someone could just pinpoint what I was going through, like that and I started to cry over the phone.

"I think there is a demon on your Facebook page. God had shown me who tried to seduce your husband." I remember that I was lying in bed at the time. It was 6 a.m. and I sat up in bed with my heart racing. "What?" I asked, "Who?"

My mentor sent me a screenshot of a young man and I was devastated. Even though I knew I could not be J's wife any longer, he had been cheating on me for a long time. She said, "I saw the vision of the man your husband was conversing with about two months ago."

I was furious. My body felt hot, and my brain was cloudy. I remember saying, "I have peace. I'm moving on." It was a lie, I was still hurt, pissed, and embarrassed because the conversion ignited all my uncontrollable feelings of insecurity.

After messaging my mentor, I couldn't stop scouring the man's picture she had sent me. I stalked his Facebook page, but we didn't have any mutual friends. J and I were no longer friends on social media so, I couldn't tell if they were friends or not. All morning, I couldn't get that man's picture out of my mind.

I didn't know what I was going to do next, but it seemed as if my emotions got the best of me. I reached out to the man and asked him if he knew J. I waited for a response for what seemed like forever. When my phone dinged, he said he didn't know J at all. On that note I dismissed everything that my mentor stated to me, and I thanked him for his time.

I moved on because I wasn't going to be on an emotional rollercoaster. As I prepared myself for a walk, my phone dinged again. The man messaged me again, "I went back to look at his page again and yes, I know him. I was introduced to him by..." The same mentor who had prophesied to me introduced them! I was crushed, I felt betrayed that she deliberately stabbed me right in my back while I looked at our reflections in the mirror. She tried to catch J in the act.

The gentleman and I continued to converse, and he showed me messages between him and my mentor. She was adamant about getting him a job through J ad luring him into the bait, knowing that her true intentions were to hurt me and my family.

I never thought that my boss, mentor, and family friend would be the same person that wanted to see me break. How can I trust anyone when people I thought loved me could violate me, lie, and want to see my world crumble? I thought my family and close friends would be supportive and encouraging but some of them were the ones wishing I fell headfirst on my face. I guess it made them feel empowered to be doing better than me.

They thought I was crumbling, but they were very wrong.

Still Smile

Today I look at you and all the memories we created,
may have been a lie, but I smile.
As I watch our children talk and play I look at you with tears in
my eyes, but I still smile.
As I look at my ring finger with no ring after 14 years of marriage
erase with a signature I still smile

- Erica Estella

After that incident I seized all communication with her. I kept my guard up and refused to talk to people because I had to learn that actions override all verbal words. I was not going to lose it all, again.

A few weeks after the drama I got notification on social media from a woman who dabbles in black magic. She told me that someone close to me had put a black spell on me. "You will not be able to be great in your life. You will continue to lose everything that you worked hard for if you don't allow me to heal you from the wicked spell."

I was like, "What the hell?" Suddenly, I have a voodoo woman in my messenger trying to remove a black spell over me. I asked her, "Who put it there?"

She stated, "Someone very close."

I told my mother what was going on with me and J, and she said, "Gal, please. The Blood of Jesus!" I then told the person that I was not interested. "I'm a child of God, covered by blood. No weapon of any kind formed against me shall prosper."

I blocked all communication from this individual and then a few days later another person appeared with a different name on my social media and started to follow me. I blocked that account as well and never again wanted to speak or entertain anything that was not beneficial to my mental and spiritual growth. God didn't put me here to fail, He didn't create me in His image and likeness to not conquer my destiny.

I had to really get my shit together because I was an emotional wreck. I isolated myself from everyone, the noise was too loud. Everyone had something to say about my marriage and my divorce.

I didn't want to hate J, so I had to grow and learn through the process alone. He may say we spoke more or got along better when we were married, but honestly, I don't care.

The grieving process was real. I was asking myself, "Was I that in love?" "Why couldn't I see what everyone else saw? "Did I just settle because he was there? I asked these questions and more because it is insane after 16 years of marriage that my husband realized that he was a gay man. The last time I checked, I don't have a penis.

"A woman's intuition never fails her, she fails it."

~Erica Estella

UNRAVELING

As I sat back and watched my life unravel, all I could do was accept my situation. I remember thinking when I was younger, "I would love to get married and not have kids. If I get divorce at least I can go through the process and not look back."

Here I was getting a divorce and watching the pain of my children. I was hurting, but I was not broken. My focus was on my survival and theirs. During this journey I was developing more patience, more understanding, more mental strength, and more emotional awareness. The divorce process was grueling, and I wanted the marriage to be over.

J wasn't making the divorce process easy. I had to be humble and wise. I understood that everything I did or said could potentially have been used as a weapon against me in the divorce proceedings. My kid's future was going to be secured through my actions and the words I spoke to this man. J is a smart, very driven man but he is "book smart," that's it.

I couldn't trust J. He had shown me through his actions that he's reckless, could lie untruthfully and do things to intentionally hurt me. His actions had caused me to feel a sense of betrayal, and I didn't want any part of him. Despite knowing him for most of my life, living with him, being married to him for nearly seventeen years, he was a stranger to me.

J was becoming someone who couldn't take full responsibility for his actions and spoke only to have his voice heard. In one of our disagreements, he had the balls to say to me, "You knew I was gay, and you still married me." He said that I forced him into our marriage. He took it upon himself to ask my parents for my hand in marriage, but I forced him. I hope sooner and later he can face the reality that he was the one untruthful and we all had to adapt to his lies.

When I was ready to start dating again, a guy told me, "Your husband made you unmarketable," meaning no man would find me attractive because I have three children. When I heard that my mouth said, "I don't care," but my heart was crushed. I wanted kids with him because I was in love with him. He knew he could never love me the way a husband is supposed to love his wife. I did not want to be alone. Having children must have made J, feel that his urge to be with a man would be erased. I'm so angry at him for taking away my choice. I could have slapped myself for all that I went through.

A woman's intuition never fails her, I'm trusting
her moving forward.

.

"I no longer planned to give my power away."

~Erica Estella

ON THE OTHER SIDE

My therapist told me, "Don't be ashamed of what you went through. Speak about it because the more you speak about your situation the more, you will heal." I truly believe that we all are the authors of our own life stories.

I wanted to heal and I wanted peace, happiness and to release resentment toward J. My plan was to be a great co-parent for our children. I no longer planned to give my power away.

I was growing and maturing through this transition. I was showing my daughters that I had lost everything that seemed normal, but I was rebuilding with God and by believing in myself. I wanted to show them to know their worth and never settle for less. Especially when the person you love doesn't love you back and doesn't protect and respect you.

I was raised by traditional Belizean parents who loved each other very much and did a great job raising all seven of their children. But on the other side of my divorce, I believe many of my family members settled for each other because they didn't want to start over with someone else. They invested too much to walk away. Many of my family members found a safe place to stay in a marriage for 10, 15, even 30 years as a badge of honor. I chose to break the curse of staying in a routine and empty marriage. I want my children to see a real, happy, marriage with two people in love.

Something that helped me get through the difficult time was a quote from Melody Beattie: "Grief is a cleansing process. It is an acceptance process. It moves us from our past , into today, and into a better future - a future free of sabotaging behaviors, a future that holds more options than our past." She wrote this prayer:

Today I will face discomfort, trusting that feelings of healing and release are on the other side. Help me, God, to feel whatever I need to feel to be whole and healthy. While I'm doing this, I will trust that I'm cared for and protected by myself, my friends, my Higher Power and the Universe.

Single Again

The dust was settling so I damn thought. On September 28, 2022, I became a single woman again. After months of therapy, mediation, sleepless nights, and stressful mourning, it was truly over. I was feeling liberated and broke after all the lawyers' fees, and the mediation.

I know for a fact I won't be going through another divorce. The financial burden, the emotional rollercoaster, and the end of a long-term relationship is mentally draining. I didn't want to raise my children under a different roof than their father. Bringing life into this world in a union is a blessing. I believe that getting divorced with children is a curse because it's the breakdown of the family. It felt like I was experiencing death while my damn ex-husband was alive and kicking.

When the divorce was final, I was feeling good. All I needed to do before I could move on for good was complete one important thing before my deadline of March 1, 2023. I needed to refinance our family home and put it solely in my name, or we had to place it on the market and my children, and I were going to have to move.

It was another hurdle that I had to try my best to jump over. I wanted to give my children the stability and comfort of a home; the only home they knew in Georgia. I wanted to make sure they were content throughout this ever-changing transition. I started the process early in November of 2022. I wanted to make sure that I could get approved for our home and afford it as well.

I had gotten my job back at the hospital and I was working there for over a year. My salary was great, and it was enough to allow me to afford nice things without the assistance of my ex-husband.

I started the process with a financial company, and it moved so slow. I should have known if I was getting approved within days, not months. I communicated with this lender, and I sent the required legal documents. I signed the loan forms for the refinance, and I was expecting approval, but the week I was supposed to close, the agency denied me because I had too many financial obligations.

I was disappointed because the company had taken so damn long with the process, giving me false hope. I didn't have time to pout, I found another lender and I told them my situation. I explained that I needed to get approved by the deadline. They ran my credit, and it was decent, but I had work to improve my credit score. There were several things in collections that needed my attention.

I tapped into my savings account and paid three major bills off. One bill remained that was for $8,000 which was for the timeshare we purchased together. It was on my credit report which was making my score low. I was so discouraged. I was doing everything in my power to give myself the chance to keep my home.

I was so stressed, and my emotions were all over the place. I didn't feel like working out because I caught myself worrying about my next move and not knowing what to expect from these lenders. So, when the lender asked for 12 months of mortgage payments I had to ask my ex for the information. The loan for the house was in his name, and he was supposably paying the mortgage.

When the lender retrieved the information via email it didn't look promising. He stated, "Due to months of late payments the house is not in good standing. Even though your name is not on the loan, it's still your property."

I was so pissed. Yet again, J had fucked me over. I forwarded him the email and stated, "Thank you for everything!" I felt chained. I was trying to achieve something for myself, and he kept pulling me back. I know now that God was trying to tell me something, but I was not hearing Him. I wanted to get the house in my name, and I was not going to stop until I did. God was the one making everything stop me in my tracks. I had to acknowledge Him.

I found a third loan officer. Yet again, I told a stranger my situation. "I need your honest opinion about me getting my home in my name. What's the best scenario?"

She stated, "Let me work on the numbers and I'll get back to you Ms. Erica." As I waited for her response, I went to plan B looking for a place to rent because I wanted to make sure we had a place to stay just in case I didn't make it to my deadline. But something told me to ask my ex-husband if I could have an extension on the house going on the market because I really wanted the kids to finish school and our son to graduate from Pre-K. To let him know I was serious I offered to pay the full mortgage.

J declined my offer. He wanted to go with the original date on the divorce decree. I proceeded with my plan to look for an apartment or a rental property until I heard from the loan officer.

I was working and planning for the next few months. It was time to reintroduce myself and introduce my kids to their roots. A trip to Belize was soon. My happiness dissipated when I received an email from J on January 26, 2023.

It was one of the worst emails he could have ever sent me. J was adamant about selling the house and moving forward with his life:

There are two options in regard to the house if your main factor is to keep the kids in the school system:

1. *You can move out, I will move back in and become the full custodial parent. You can sign over your deed to me so I can become full owner of our residence.*

2. *You can stay in the house and pay rent to me. Sign over your deed to me and when you are ready to buy the house you can, but it will be at market value.*

Both options remove you from ownership of the property which is necessary for the divorce. My only concern is the kids, avoiding uprooting them if I can, and not removing them from the district. We are open for discussion.

Best,
Him, Ph.D., MPA

I looked at my email for a few hours even after I responded to his ass. I couldn't believe what he was asking me to do. I know from that email it was all about his gain and having power over me knowing I was having a hard time getting approved for the loan. I was not surprised by his antics anymore. His words and actions no longer affected me. Here is my response:

MY EX-HUSBAND,

I move out, you move in becoming legal custodian of the children. Still about you not wanting to pay child support? Is this really about the children? If I turn over the deed to you, when I do that you can sell the house without warning. If I rent from you then you want me to purchase the house for full price "market value," not what is owed? I don't mind paying the mortgage starting February 1, but I'm not signing over the deed to you. You can move back in, there are five bedrooms here, have a pick.

WHERE I GO OUR CHILDREN WILL GO. I AM A FAITHFUL, GOD-BELIEVING, HANDS ON, EDUCATED, WOKE WOMAN. I WILL FIGHT FOR MY CHILDREN AND WHAT IS RIGHTFULLY THEIRS and MINE.

Have a good night.

P.S. Your only concern is money. If your concern were our children the mortgage would have been paid and the water bill would have never been disconnected after 10 months of nonpayment. Move forward and let your words and your actions be parallel so I can have some faith in you through ACTIONS.

When I sent that email, I didn't feel good. I wanted to keep my house. I couldn't eat, my stomach was in knots, I couldn't sleep, and I didn't even want to work. When I looked at my children, I truly felt that I failed them in this sense of not being able to stay in our home, to give them the security I was hoping to provide after the divorce. I worked so hard by focusing on our future and overcoming all the pain I was dealt these past years.

I conceded to the fact that my kids and I had to move without their father but it was making me anxious. I started preparing to move and pack up my family. I cleaned up the house and started looking for a place to live. I was preparing to uproot my children yet again in less than a three-year span.

Everything was falling on me. I was feeling the pressure all over my extremities, if I didn't control it, it would consume me. I started praying more asking God for clarity and to not hate that man, I just need help to understand why he couldn't just give me the house so our kids can have their inheritance, the beautiful happy ever after home in Roswell.

I know he wanted to hurt me. I admit that he gave us our amazing forever home, but our money purchased it from the sale of our previous home in California. J left us and moved on with his new life.

He never asked if I needed help with anything from changing a light bulb to replacing the dryer which had been broken for two years after we moved into our home. He didn't care about that or any other thing that impacted us. We weren't his priority.

With his god-like attitude, J made it seem that he had everything under control when he didn't have anything but his degrees and debt. He didn't have love, he didn't have dignity, and he surely didn't have common sense.

THE BEGINNING OF THE END

Our forever home went on the market on March 1, 2023. Every time I saw the "For Sale" sign in front of my home I felt vulnerable. It hurt me that this man couldn't give his children stability, especially when I agreed to start paying the mortgage on the house.

My heart hurt with the prospect of losing my dream home. I didn't know why I couldn't get the house in my name. I made several attempts and asked several financial institutions to assist but I was denied. I didn't have any other choice but to sell when J refused to give me more time to refinance.

The day was drawing near for our closing. I was nervous and excited because I was ready to close this chapter completely and the funds from the sale would be able to pay off debt and save for the purchase of my home.

When my realtor sent the documents of the closing and the payout, I was not going to receive what I expected. It was $75,000 short because J had taken out a second mortgage on the house and did not tell me. I asked him several times when I was trying to refinance the house in my name, and he was dishonest. That lie made me fucking mad. I couldn't believe I had put up with him for so many years under the guise of love.

I needed to tap into my faith because I was being tested to the 10th degree. I listened to the Word of God to prevent me from exploding on J for jeopardizing my future and the future of our children. He took so much from me and never apologized. I couldn't forgive J for lying about the house. How could I trust a word he said to me?

I was losing everything that I worked hard for.

My marriage was dead, my income taxes were seized because he owed taxes, and my home was being sold because I could not refinance it in my name. It felt like someone was standing on my chest and I couldn't exhale the mess I was inhaling. I started to work my ass off after the divorce to give my children stability and normalcy. I found a house in the same neighborhood and school system, and I was excited about it. This was my first time living alone and damn, I was scared and nervous, all wrapped up like a sushi roll.

I was walking into my new chapter bold; not broken. I was being refined.

REFINED

I was taught that when you have issues in your marriage keep it in the marriage, but I was never taught that if your marriage is killing you spiritually who to turn to? My divorce affected everyone that knew and loved us together, as #CoupleGoals.

From the time of my marriage to signing divorce papers, I have gained a lot of knowledge on how to truly love myself. I now know how to love someone with actions not just verbal. I will never get too comfortable again. I will be alert and protect my finances so that I won't be hostage to anyone, not even myself.

Because of my divorce I have started praying more. I started to write poetry, started working out and slowly revitalized my life even more to release the anger that was building up inside me. I also loved going to therapy.

My therapist has taught me how to be observant with an individual's actions and listen to their words. I've learned to self-reflect because pointing fingers won't allow me to reach my full potential. I will not allow my actions to consume me. I will own my words in order to grow from them. I also learned that I want a mate who can pray with and for me, protect me, love me, admit their wrongs, respect me, and communicate when things aren't feeling right.

Be Honest With Your Children

Children are resilient. The announcement that that their father is gay, to the divorce, my children have been through a lot. It was a huge adjustment for them to learn about the sexuality of their father than to have him move out of the family home. I was afraid of failing them. I had to survive, and it took prayer, mental, emotional, and spiritual guidance.

I am the legal custodial parent of our children, and they tell me how they feel. They love their father, and they would rather see him happy than express their true feelings of hurt and abandonment. The sad thing is that J will not apologize to them. If he did, he would have to hold himself accountable for his actions. I know he's not going to do that shit.

Our youngest gave me the good, the bad and the ugly one day he said, "I want to live with dad because I love him more." Our youngest daughter told me that she doesn't like me. They don't give their dad the disrespect and mess they give me because they don't want to hurt his feelings.

Our oldest daughter stated, "Everything we went through from the time dad said he is gay, to us losing our house, is his fault. I know what's going on Mommy, I know." Unfortunately, she will never tell him how she feels.

Go To Therapy

In my first two therapy sessions all I did was cry. I couldn't really communicate with her. My therapist helped me open about my marriage and my personal self-development. When I finally started talking about my life and the process of my divorce, she helped me understand that the situation is not my fault. "Don't be ashamed of the divorce," she reassured me. "Communicating about your life will help you heal and grow in all areas of your life.

Affirm Yourself

It took me months to realize my worth again. Looking in the mirror I didn't see what others saw, I saw myself lonely, rejected, and desperate. I had to put into work my affirmations and scriptures to relearn self-love and self-worth.

I started to take care of myself physically by walking again. I started going out, dressing to feel alive and better, and going to the gym more. I felt at that moment that being healthy was vital for the healing process. My healing was just a piece of what I needed to do to accept my situation and truly release any negativity I had toward myself and toward him.

I spoke affirmations over my life and I played two songs on repeat for months "Why Not Me," and "Praise in the Middle." Those songs carried me through most of the rough part of 2021 and still affirm me today.

Walk Into the Unknown

At one time I was afraid to walk into the unknown. I was comfortable with what was familiar and that held me hostage. I'm here to tell you, do not be scared to close a bad chapter of your life. Growth came from becoming uncomfortable and walking through those doors to the unknown, taking those steps into your rebirth.

During the process of finalizing my divorce, we marked 16 years of marriage. I was in denial that the marriage was even ending. I tried to block out what was happening because my mind didn't want to accept it. I grieved because my husband didn't want me, but I still wanted him and our family.

I was depressed for months. People may have seen me smiling when I was working and being attentive to my kids, but deep down inside I was fragile. I didn't want to live because I was embarrassed, and I felt worthless due to my failed marriage.

There was so much I kept inside, away from my family and friends because I was abandoned again—first it was my father, then it was my ex-husband. I felt alone and ashamed. I continue to attend church, where we were both very active. He was on the Praise and Worship team, and I was involved with the Women's Ministry and Bible Study. Part of me wanted to give up my faith, I didn't want to face reality or the people who were questioning me about my ex-husband. I did not read my bible or go to church during the process. I felt that I was not worthy to talk to God about my life, my journey or my situation. I really felt that I had failed HIM.

I questioned God and my faith. I felt alone without God, I wanted my faith, I wanted my peace and the only way to receive that is to release all my mess to Him in prayer. I wanted to be renewed in body and spirit, but I couldn't do that by myself or with my therapist. Only my faith in GOD would allow me to see the vision He set forth for my life. I had to make it my foundation for elevation, not my deprivation.

My worst fear became a reality when I was dropping off some clothes at the thrift store. I ran into a church member who recognized me. He said, "Hello, how's everything? How's your husband?"

There it goes. "We are separated," I responded.

He was shocked, "Wow! You are beautiful together, what happened?"

Bam! There was the question everyone wanted an answer to even me. I wasn't ready to give all my emotions to that church member, a stranger who didn't even know my name, but wanted the breakdown of my marriage.

I already couldn't look at myself in the mirror and accept the fact that my husband abandoned us. My therapist kept telling me, "Erica you are not the problem, stop blaming yourself for that broken man that tried to break you."

The process of marriage and divorce has changed me. I'm not Erica who married her high school sweetheart. I'm not Erica who walked down the aisle to marry her knight in shining armor. I'm not the same woman who had three beautiful children and relocated her life to support her husband's dreams.

I have been refined into a new woman who is more resilient, eager to survive, thirsty to flourish and living in her truth for herself and her children.

My story is the same as so many of you. There are many of us who have gotten married and stayed in long-term relationships because we were afraid of the unknown that starting over would bring. Maybe we were hoping that eventually things would get better. Maybe we kept going and stayed for roses, wine, and the hope of amazing sex.

I'm still waiting for an apology and a conversation as to why J married me knowing he was a homosexual man. I will never get those conversations so I'm not holding my breath. At the end of the day, I want us to start the new chapter of our lives knowing that it is God that will elevate us.

The reality is that we knew we weren't what our partner truly wanted. We tried our best to do things and endure in our relationship, but now we question if it was even worth it. I looked at life through that lens for many years. For the years approaching, I need to truly listen to my heart, the soul wearing the lens, there are things only the blind can see and the deaf can hear.

I had a moment when I thought that the divorce broke me, and I now realize that I am not a failure. I was never broken; but under construction longer to be refined. To be refined means that I can do things that I didn't know could do. I walked away from a marriage of almost 20 years, I love myself more than ever and I know my worth.

I am not her any longer. I am feeling renewed and alive as I walk in my purpose on the other side of divorce. The fight that I have to survive shows my worth and my resilience. I did not lose this fight, but I gained self-awareness and now I trust myself enough to push myself to greater heights and speak up when I feel something does not "sit right" or settle in my spirit.

Woman in Me

You will never break the warrior, the provider,
the child of GOD,
that blessed you with many years of love and sacrifices
I am not Broken just Refined

- Erica Estella

REFERENCES

Elle, Alexandra. *How We Heal: Uncover Your Power and Set Yourself Free Hardcover* (2022)

MOMENTS OF REFINEMENT

In *Not Broken: Just Refined* the author discusses some delicate subjects. She suggests that you gather with a group of sisters, friends, church sisters, or accountability partners to read this book together and discuss it in a confidential, safe setting.

Use the following questions as conversation starters to help you, and your group look for the refining moments in your life after brokenness.

- Would you have stayed in the marriage if your spouse came out to you?
- Talk about a time when you felt broken. How did you overcome that feeling?
- If you had a friend who was experiencing this kind of situation, what would you do to support them in getting through it?
- How would you cope with your children's adjustment if their parent came out?
- Why do you think the author's husband did not want to reveal his true self?
- What does it mean to be refined?

- Like Hagar in the Bible, at what point do you think Erica Estella realized she was ready to let go of her marriage?
- Like Vashti in the Bible, how does the author model what it means to walk in her worthiness?

SONGS OF REFINEMENT

I told you about two songs that carried me through most of the rough part of 2021: "Why Not Me" by Tasha Paige Lockhart and "In the Middle" by Isaac Caree. I still go back to these songs because they affirm me to this day

Make a list of some your favorite worship songs.

NOT BROKEN
Just Refined

ABOUT THE AUTHOR

Erica Estella is from Los Angeles, California. The daughter of Belizean parents, she was raised in a loving, but strict household where she learned, "If you want it, work for it."

Erica has been in healthcare for over 20 years and owns BreathPulseCompress LLC, and is the primary instructor of Basic Life Support (BLS), Cardiac Pulmonary Resuscitation, CPR for healthcare workers and the public. She has a passion to help people to make a difference. Additionally, she owns H-Teamgems, a business with fantastic and reasonably priced Paparazzi Jewelry. As a business owner, Erica is building financial stability and has found a way to get through difficult seasons. Crediting her three beautiful children and her businesses for helping her heal , Erica seeks to share her rebirthing and healing process in her first book, *Not Broken, Just Refined.*

Using her platform as a social media influencer, Erica provides hope, education, encouragement, and prayers to women who have, or are going through a divorce, as well as guidance on how to rebuild their lives. She says, "Remember sis, you are still standing and have a mission to continue growing."

www.ingramcontent.com/pod-product-compliance
Lightning Source LLC
Chambersburg PA
CBHW051206120626
46547CB00013B/1227